Bull Buffalo
and
Indian Paintbrush

(The Poetry of Oklahoma)

Edited by
Ron Wallace

Copyright © 2020 by TJMF Publishing
In Association with Buffalo Press
Durant, Oklahoma
Cover Design by Jim Furber
Edited by Ron Wallace

Second Printing

Printed and Bound in the United
States by Publisher's Graphics, LLC
ISBN Number: 978-0-9910671-5-2
Library of Congress Number: 2020903707

Notes from the Editor

"How This Book Came To Be"

Forty-something years ago I was a converted pre-law student becoming an English major at Southeastern Oklahoma State University when I encountered a culmination of two voices, both belonging to men of genius.

Howard Starks was one of the professors I had come to respect and admire. Dennis Letts was another, and one day in class I heard Dennis, in that magnificent voice of his, which should have been on Broadway decades before it was, reading one of Howard's poems, which should have been widely published across the country, and the effect was profound. I had discovered poetry, real poetry.

It was not the rhyming, metered verse of Shakespeare, Shelley, Byron or Keats, all of whom I admired and enjoyed. It was a voice not too unlike mine. Howard wrote Oklahoman and Dennis made it echo like Native drums beating a rhythm that I knew so well.

I have often said that was the moment I discovered that I wanted to become a poet. Whether it actually was or that is a romanticized memory, doesn't really matter. Whether it took days, weeks, months or years for that understanding to fully blossom, it did flower and grow in my mind. I am still trying to become a poet, and I know that these voices led me to other voices over the next four decades, voices that speak of all things Oklahoma: its good and its bad, its joy and its brutality, it's intellect and its ignorance.

So... this book is for them. Any profit it might miraculously see (every nickel) will go into an existing scholarship at Southeastern with hope that new poets will arise from the voices of Oklahoma, this relatively small place, which occupies the hearts of a multitude of beings: cowboys, Indians, philosophers, ballplayers, actors, singers, teachers, astronauts, pilgrims, prophets, and poets... especially poets.

Within these pages, you'll find the most celebrated authors alongside emerging voices of Oklahoma poets. They cover a span of decades and reflect the changing views of Oklahoma; all offer the language, the heart and the voice of the state itself, that same state which gave of the likes of Woody Guthrie, Will Rogers and Ralph Ellison.

Maybe there's something in the water, or maybe it's in those blue skies, those stars that shine like no others, those Okie drawls soft as dirt in a rodeo arena. Whatever it is, I hope these poems offer a value to the reader and a fair representation of the artistry.

I hope that the eclectic voices of these writers join with the hawk, the bison, the coyote, the cattle, the horse herds, and that infamous wind that comes sweeping down the plains to sing in a sacred choir, spiritual, honest, sometimes irreverent, but irrevocably honest.

Table of Contents

Voices

Well, I've never been to Heaven, but I've been to Oklahoma.
Hoyt Axton

When the Okies left Oklahoma and moved to California, it raised the I.Q. of both states.
Will Rogers

Many a month has come and gone since I wandered from my home in those Oklahoma hills where I was born.
Woody Guthrie

Anything can have happened in Oklahoma. Practically everything has.
Edna Ferber

I'd rather be a lover than a fighter of wars, be from Oklahoma than the nebulous stars.
Hoyt Axton

With the exception of my wife and children, there's nothing I value more than my Oklahoma heritage.
James Garner

One day in Landfill, Oklahoma, is worth more to me than an eternity in Dante's plastic Paradiso, or Yeats's gold-plated Byzantium.
Edward Abbey

This is the Plains (Oklahoma): a state of mind, right, some spiritual affliction, like the Blues.
Tracy Letts

Resilience is woven deeply into the fabric of Oklahoma.
Brad Henry

I'm from Oklahoma. I mean you can't have good hair in Oklahoma. The wind just messes it up. That's why everyone wears hats.

Ronnie Dunn

Oh, honey, I'm from Oklahoma! This is who I am – middle class all the way!

Annette Bening

I used to limp around my neighborhood imitating Mickey Mantle. I did my Bar Mitzvah with an Oklahoma drawl.

Billy Crystal

I grew up in southeastern Oklahoma on a working cattle ranch, and it was always romantic to me: The West, the cowboy, the Western way of life.

Reba McEntire

Okies – the owners hated them because they knew they were soft and the Okies strong...

John Steinbeck

I feel as if I'm a child again, watching an Oklahoma thunderstorm gathering in the distance, anticipating its wonder, yet fearing its potential and loving every minute of it.

Garth Brooks

The Last Song ~ Joy Harjo

how can you stand it
he said
the hot oklahoma summers
where you were born
this humid thick air
is choking me
and i want to go back
to new mexico

it is the only way
i know how to breathe
an ancient chant
that my mother knew
came out of a history
woven from wet tall grass
in her womb
and i know no other way
than to surround my voice
with the summer songs of crickets
in this moist south night air

oklahoma will be the last song
i'll ever sing

Sunday Morning Photograph ~ Howard Starks

Most days
he had an easy Daddy smell
   Prince Albert smokes
   man sweat
   P and G soap
   and the waxy musk
   denim of the oil he worked in
and his chambray shirt
and Penney's overalls
 were (silky) with long wear
   soft

Now| |he has a Sunday smell
   of Faultless starch
    hot irons
    and rosy brilliantine

When you're dressed up| |he says
     your clothes wear you
  and ours are wearing us
but we are grand in snowy shirts
        starched linen pants
  and strange new shoes

I am loved| |prized| |and know it
I claim his knee
  as mine by right
     son
   young lord

TRANQUILLITY ~ Louis L'Amour

I wander down along the oak-clad hills
   Where twilight lives beneath the tranquil trees,
   Along dim aisles untouched by passing breeze,
Where perfume that the violet distills
Becomes the essence of the shade, and fills
   With fragrance all the gloomy corridor –
I walk along the shadowed forest floor
And think of things that solitude instills.
No sound disturbs the fading afternoon
   As mellow dreams come drifting down the years,
   Remembered thoughts, a half-forgotten tune –
An endless chain of hopes, and smiles, and tears;
   So turning from almost forgotten ills,
   I wander back along the oak-clad hills.

Originally published in <u>Smoke from This Altar</u>
Published here with permission from Katherine L'Amour

An Oklahoma Litany ~ Wilma Elizabeth McDaniel

Top drawers of the memory
   never contain
   any healing for me
When wounded
   I always pull out
   the bottom drawer
   of my memory
   the one marked Oklahoma
It holds a list of old towns
with funny names and touching beauty
   which I recite with reverence
   Bowlegs
   Depew
   Pretty Water
   Idabel
      Lone Star
      Gypsy Corner
   Broken Arrow
   Cloud Chief
      until the words
      form a prayer
which I do not understand
   but I close the drawer
   with my own Amen

From Wilma Elizabeth McDaniel: Oklahoma Poet, Daughter of Great Depression and Dust Bowl Emigrant, California Okie Poet and Storyteller, 2013. Courtesy University of California, Merced Library. Copyright owned by the Regents of the University of California.

Open Container   ~ Jim Spurr

Before he died in 1953 at age 39,
Dylan Thomas left a beer can on the podium
at Oklahoma University on his last USA tour.

Anyhow that's the story I was told as we sat by
a wood burning stove down the road a piece
from a small honkeytonk near Pink, Oklahoma.
Just two of us. She was there. Had witnessed it all.
She said.

Here's her story:
Thomas was drunk and everyone put up with it
because he was a great poet and a known genius.
The beer brand was Falstaff, she said.
Popular brand at the time. Named, we assume,
after the pleasure-seeking Shakespearean
only a mother or a drunkard could love.
It had church key openings, which preceded the
aluminum vinyl age of timesaving flip top devices.
The drama department enshrined it. Then later,
when a new theater was built, it got stolen.
Anyway it was gone.

I believed her, and here's my story:
I'd like to own that can or an exact duplicate.
Then lie about where I got it
so I could stand up in some isolated bar
in Anywhere, U.S.A. and quote, "Wild men
who caught and sang the sun in flight...
(then some other line I forgot)
do not go gentle into that good night."

The Land ~ N. Scott Momaday

The first person to enter upon it
Must have given it a name, wind-borne
   and elemental
Like summer rain.
The name must have given spirit to the land,
For so it is with names.
Before the first people there must have been
The profound isolation of night and day,
The blazing shield of the sun,
The darkness winnowed from the stars –
The holy havoc of myth and origin,
True and prophetic, and inexorable,
Like summer rain.

What was to become of the land?
What was the land to become?
What was there in the land to define
The falling of the rain and the turning of the seasons,
The far and forever silence of the universe?

A voice, a name,
Words echoing the whir of wings
Swelled among the clouds
And sounded on the red earth in the wake
   of creation.
A voice. A name.
Oklahoma.

Cimarron ~ Ken Hada

A wildness that will not fade
calls in the crimson twilight.

Our tangled roots of dirt and desire and denial
are embedded in cyclical rhythms linked
to the full moon shining
over Cherokee County, pulling
the Cimarron River along to the Arkansas,
filtering sand from clay, leaving
the heron a feast, the mallard a respite.

Survivors know these rhythms –
these voices calling out in wild red darkness.

from The Way of the Wind
(Morris, OK: Fine Dog Press, 2019)

Redland IV ~ Carol Hamilton

Blackjack oaks go nobbing and humping eastward,
Recreating themselves as they go,
Searching out higher hills and rain
Beyond where the vapor trail stops the sun,
Captures a bit of light, and makes tracks.
To the west even the scrub oak
Lose heart, give out to the aridity.
Creekside arbors bend low in deference
To the south wind. Downward off
The Rockies the state slopes from high
Flatlands to low mountains, a paradox.
We walk tipped against the wind
And the great continental fold,
Against the scorching and
The icy gales, caught in extremes.
Survivors need room to move about
Where extinction carves out space.

Originally published in Greensboro Review

Quail Hunt, One-Horse, OK, 1982

~ Benjamin Myers

The Johnson grass is <u>like</u> a yellow flame
beneath a thin glass dome. My grandfather
this morning wades into that fire, *imagery*
his 20 gauge draped open in the crook
of his elbow, like a bird he's already shot.
I follow his orange plaid hunting jacket
through waist-high blades of scouring, blonded grass
to pet the dog he's brought for nosing up
the birds from bare and brushy upwards rush
of scrub. I know by the time we cross
this frozen creek again the shells he's spent
will bulge my pocket like a bullfrog's throat.
This man was born before this land was a state
and now begins to knee his way into
the high grass of his last ten years, not yet
frail, not yet waning down to elbow
and kneecap on a hospice bed, still strong
as cedar root in hard red earth. The dog
noses a sudden flash of bobwhites up,
like a handful of dirt clods flung
against the cold clear dome of pre-snow sky.
And some may say to shoot them down is brutal,
but I already know that, in a place
that's mostly sky, to shoot a bird back down
to earth is just a way to keep the rest
of all we've got from rising to follow
and <u>falling up</u> toward that dead-cold,
forever distant, cracked and bluish dome.

the sky, heaven

Originally appeared in the San Pedro River Review

Sunday in the Wichitas ~ Sandra Soli

from England

Here at the top of Mount Scott
visitors can spot five lakes and two states
if weather's not hazy. Down on the right
the Lawtonka boathouse where we sat
on the roof that summer, me kissing you
not for love then but for your love of stars,
naming them. To the north, a bluff
where Geronimo and his horse leaped
into Apache sky, escaping time and again
until finally, plumb weary, drifting in
like smoke for the safety of a cell—
three squares and fame but watched,
a fox refused its dignity. Flying off
a mountain was myth, we knew
but given one sprint up into Big Dog,
the canicular boot of the night, just once
is all a warrior needs to make it true.

Storyteller ~ Jeanetta Calhoun Mish

For Louisa Ellen Exendine Sanderson

I drive toward the arms of the Canadian River,
it calls to me, jealous of the Hudson *going home*
murmuring through my window
through long winter nights.

reincarnated

In Oklahoma an owl waits silently
amid the rubble of my grandmother's house.
Her face shines out from its eyes,
its wings brush the cracked edges of memory.

The tires hum, an intermittent rain [sequins] the
windshield,
a shy moon hides behind a veil of black clouds. *the night*
Radio stations fade in and out with the passing miles
and an urgent wind impels me westward. *driven*

Grandmother,
you were silenced before you could
begin to tell me the stories;
I am coming home.
I am listening everywhere
for your voice.

Originally published in "Work Is Love Made Visible"
West End Press-Albuquerque, New Mexico 2009

I Ask My Father to Sing   ~ Dorothy Alexander

At the Senior Living Center
I ask my father to sing us a song.
He sits up straight like a schoolboy
and begins an old Jimmy Rodgers tune,
'Just Waitin' for a Train.'

Now, I've never been a thousand miles
from home without a penny to my name.
Never been kicked off a train in Texas,
nor slept out in the rain. But I like to hear
him sing it in his quavering old voice.

When he sees my tears, he reaches for his
harmonica and says, "Let's have something
cheerful. How about an Irish jig?"

If my mother were still alive, she would shake
her head and say, "He never could carry a tune."

Hang Me in the Tulsa County Stars
~ John Moreland

Hang me in the Tulsa County stars.
Meet me where I land if I slip and fall too far.
Hang me in the Tulsa County stars.

I don't want to come back down to earth.
My heart is growing heavy from the ever-endless hurt,
so I don't want to come back down to earth

I know this life will make you cold and leave you mad,
make you homesick for a home you never had,
burning out the good with all the bad

So, let the charmers leave the room;
they're drowning out the Nashville moon.
I want to learn exactly who you are.

Find me in the Indian Nation sky.
When it feels like nothing's real and no one's standing
on your side,
just find me in the Indian Nation sky.

I know this world will have the wolves outside your
door,
make you leave all that you love to fight a war,
and never tell you what you're dying for.
Just hang me in the Tulsa County stars.

Excerpt from the song "Hang Me in the Tulsa County Stars"
by John Moreland used with permission of Thomas Young, TT
Management.

nightfall ~ Paul Austin

leave the lamp unlit,
unclose the window curtain,
look beyond the glass.

can you not feel
the uninhabited night
pulsing with desire?

can you not hear
the blue anticipation
murmuring to you?

let loose your heart's fear,
give of your eyes to vastness,
that it may be seen.

Sashay

Some people can sashay their long necks
side to side to glide their words as they talk,
others—in thrall to frolic and flounce—
sashay their hips this way and that
as they swan and swagger,
and supposed experts can sashay
hypotheticals ad infinitum
in quest of credentials,
some sashay by rolling their eyes
in the presence of pathological liars
and who has not seen an infant
in its crib sashay its entire body
when tickled.

THE HILLTOP BAR ~ Sly Alley

It was the kinda place
you could shoot a few
games of pool.
If you timed it right you could
have 4 or 6 beers
under that framed painting
of a naked white woman
and get out
before the late-nighters
came in looking to get crazy.
In the fall you could see the sun sink
down behind Tecumseh from the parking lot.

It was the kinda place
the 14 or 25 churches
in town probably weren't happy
about having just outside the city limits.

But that cinder block walled
beer bar
has been closed
for a while now.
Rumor around town
is that the police department
bought it.
And I'm thinking
about joining the force
just to see
if that framed painting
is still hanging over the bar.

TARZAN in the OSAGE ~ *Bill McCloud*
(and the rickety bridge)

Early 60s my early teens
I spent summers
with my grandparents
out in the Osage

playing with horny toads
avoiding scorpions
enjoying the fruit of
the watermelon fields

listening to Cardinals baseball
on the radio and reading the
complete set of Tarzan books
in red hard covers that my
grandpa bought me at a sale

I know now I learned patience
from my grandparents
as the melons grew or
as we waited our chance
at the party line or our
visit to the outhouse

and all the times we waited
for our turn to cross
the old one-lane bridge
we'd travel during
trips into town
The long rickety bridge
that seemed to have a
life of its own and a
desire to take mine

and scared me more than I ever
dared let my grandpa know

So I said a silent prayer each time
our old pickup moved onto the
bridge and I opened my book
and went in search of
the Jewels of Opar

This Is the Time of Year ~ Sharon Edge Martin

A country girl starts each day
with a ritual,
geranium oil, or whatever is in fashion,
rubbed on ankles, arms, neck.
Socks are required. No sandals
out here. She lies to herself,
maybe even believes
that the ticks, chiggers, mosquitos,
the tiny biting gnats, for heaven's sake,
won't get her this time

as she heads out to count the chickens
tomato blossoms,
and her blessings, among which
is a daily handful of blackberries,
each berry as big as her thumb,
sweet, juicy,
decadent.

MILITARY BURIAL, SUMMERFIELD CEMETERY, A LATE EULOGY ~ Jim Barnes

In Memoriam J. C. Evans

An honor guard brought the gray box down from
Tinker Field the day of burial. A few
Of us came up the hill as if we knew
This man death and the flyers carried home.

How easy it is when you are nine or ten
To let your body go into the night,
Into a dream of glory that's just right
For you. When you are nineteen and a man,

The dream is still a dream but need is there.
Over fifty years have gone since they lowered
Him to this still place, his wings of sculptured
Granite now aloft in an angelic air.

I remember echoes in the woods: the sound
Of Taps soft in the late afternoon sun,
The stilling volley, the ceremony done.
Deranged by time I felt the trees around

The drab cemetery shudder in the light
Wind rising in the clear south, and from
The west I heard a high plane's engines thrum.
Now it is hard to name what his last flight

Was for: honor, glory, right, or just war.
Others have ended near him, on this hill,
From later skies. For all who had the will
For wings I give these words I wish were more.

*from Sundown Explains Nothing: New and Selected Poems
(Stephen F. Austin State University Press, 2019)*

Dumplins ~ Jessica Isaacs
for Cori

Now it was just a memory
of broth, flour, and sunshine sifting
through her kitchen curtains
and landing on her hands;
Nanny was teaching us,
her eldest granddaughters,
how to make chicken and dumplins
on her propane stove.
    "First you must flour your hands,"
                    she said,

and I remember
the June wind fluttering
through her yellow cotton curtains
like dragonflies
as we scattered the flour
across our hands, smearing it
across our tea-towel aprons,
and getting it in our hair.
    "Don't forget the Crisco,"
                    she warned,
scooping out the measure by hand,

        "you've got to get down in there
            and use a lot of Crisco—
            and salt —" she said,
        "you always need more salt than you think.
            Now, girls, flour that counter,
            flour your rolling pins, work it in,
            make the dough thin, but not too thin,"
                she corrected,

sprinkling us with her laughter,
as we floured the counter
next to her kitchen sink
where she used to lay us out
to wash our hair years ago
when we were much smaller,
and now, we rolled out the dough together,
Nanny's hands showing us
how to create nourishment from nothing,
loving us as she dropped bits of dough
into boiling broth, teaching us

to feel the tender pull of the dough,
the right time of the boil,
as light and warm
as the June sun

Originally published in Oklahoma Today

Choices ~ Richard Dixon

In Berry House I became aware
there were two avenues of direction
I could be going

an institution like the Baptist Boys Ranch
or placement in a foster home
against the former but willing
to roll the dice on foster care

Two months passed before I was taken
to the country outside Oklahoma City
where, if I assented, I'd meet my future
foster parents and their daughter

Once finalized but before
my departure, a counselor told me
if I stayed two more days there
I would own the new record
for longest stay, currently held
by a ten-year old psycho-delinquent
who set fire to a Texaco refinery
with millions in damages

I thought about this as only
a kid might, decided
I had done all the damage
I could stand

Originally appeared in Leaving Home
WJB Publishing 2017

A Place Called Oklahoma ~ Chuck Ladd

Scientists and such people say
certain colors of the sky *I love the sky*
are due to something called
meteorological conditions "

(association)
but my ancestors say that blue sky
is a sign of peaceful spirits
and gray troubled clouds sing of a
threatened heart
and rain is a tear gift of my people.
relation, understanding

Weathermen say that a red sky
is some meteorological trick
of reflection refraction and light
puncuation

but weather gods say a red sky
is the ascended blood of my ancestors
who settled in
a place called Oklahoma.

Originally appeared in My Granddaughter Paints
TJMF Publishing 2019

Ponca ~ John Yozzo

The Arkansas and its dredge-piles
are not easily forgotten haunts.
hours after the scoops were tethered
we hauled blankets and ice chest
to riverside symposia. fortified
by Coors, emboldened by nightfall
we would skinny dip the brown waters.
I stole glimpses of a girl too forward,
thinking to plant herself too small

where Standing Bear a century ago stood
to muse "I gotta get outta this place"
I was planted and tonight I finally can appreciate
the limits of this sheltered prairie town
this rural air unlike the cities' casserole
the benzene tang of our refineries assures
skies here are yet clear, and traffic actual
and metaphorical less dense
and amiable

Originally published in <u>Echoes and Omens</u>
Village Books Press, Cheyenne, Ok, 2019

December ~ Paul Bowers

While the horses dishevel
the round hay bale

a winter fog rides careless
upon their backs

until a mid-morning breeze
unsaddles the mist

and those ragged souls,
upended, depart.

On Witnessing a Farmer Plowing a New Field in Spring, Major County, Oklahoma

How you scribe the earth
how you slow its spin by increments
how you gouge the past
and roil it up again

that ragged history in soil
those remembrances of rain
and drought, eons only inches deep

speaking in rows of curling hillocks
a rope of clenched fists
and mounded beliefs

that score of knotted notes
played by an iron needle
when singing time comes.

Dear Hank, ~ Nathan Brown
(for Hank Jones)

Moving to Oklahoma
implies a degree of intent.

Retired Jewish doctors or,
say, Italian police officers
from New York do not
wake up some weird day
and decide to move here
from Boca Raton or, say,
St. Petersburg, Florida,
because the summers
are so nice... and...
the winters so mild.

Californians will never
even know what is here,
because they all get stuck
along the way in the flytraps
that are Sedona and Santa Fe.
At the same time, we are quite
content not to have them, no?

Our friends from the Upper
Peninsula in Michigan, who
just moved down to Texas,
didn't even know that they
had passed through here,
somewhere after St. Louis.

So, if you've landed in Oklahoma,
you're taking the backroads to heaven,
the slower and quieter route—the one
not everybody gets to see, my friend.

"In Every Sense"

Oklahoma may not seep
into, and invade, the marrow
of your bones the way it did mine.

No, it's not for everyone... true.
Which explains the population.

But there are tints and hues,
lurking among the purples,
the pinks and the oranges
of these big-sky sunsets,
not seen anywhere else.
The breezes prowl deep
and make a soft purring
sound in the tallgrasses
of these high prairies
I've only heard here.

The smell of damp oak
burning in wet Decembers
breaks my heart all to hell.

And, this will always be
the only place I've ever
tasted my mother's fresh-
baked homemade bread.

This holy land, for me,
is God-finger on bone,
turning me ever so slowly,
and faithfully, into ashes.

Exactly where... I hope...
they will, someday, return.

Oklahoma Today - Larry Griffin
for Bill Fogelman

What then, the moon high in the Osage sky,
a long done sun and then the Moon Dog
there within the nation, then no Wilson
finds himself so far away from his home.

I adore the whispers of the bay windows
and how the breeze in the far out loom
of creed shakes the foundation of this
Oklahoma house after decades of earth

quakes, a canyon secret of hollow flat
bitter orchard, some peaches never put
up, jars never sealed, eclectic whispers
of wires to span the skies so pallid blue,

and all that talk then of me and of you.
Not the hymns, but he's of all the her's,
whatever then did finally after all shut
the bark of dog and the last meow of cat

before the frown's last laughter of birth
or crawl of lizard. Just then a snake's hiss
makes its ample moment in this room
there among afternoon purple shadows,

when I had no other range then to roam,
out of any ration, no other place to run,
no other fish to catch, no gig for frog,
but I ask this one last question, "

Work ~ Rilla Askew

My mother knew when I did not,
when I thought it just a stick
across the path, and if we'd traded
sides it could have bit me had it
been the kind of snake that bit.
But Mama knew, and Oh! she said,
and hardly jumped. Is that a snake?
And I said, No, then, Yes, because
I saw it then (and still it thought it
could pretend to not be itself)
while Mama turned along
the purpling path and hurried
back beside the gate
to get her hoe.

I told that snake, said, Ssst,
ssst, you'd best git back,
she'll hack you dead. It didn't
git but stayed, a seeming stick
across the road. It tried
to fool this woman who
could not be fooled
until it sensed the hoe
blade coming down, it
whipped to run, too late.
She got its tail in weeds enough
to bloody keep it pinned to earth,
and sawed and hacked
and whacked with hoe,
the snakeflesh curled
like Satan's breath.

My mom and I went on.

Our dusking walk near finished,
we turned back, and saw the barn cat
paw the path and, leaping back,
touch paw again. I knew that snake
was writhing still. We paused
and Mama, looking, said, it's dead,
and went on to the house.
But me, a northern transplant
who has lost all sense and
cannot tell dead stick from
snake without my mother's eyes
to see, but me, who'll eat no flesh
that walks on legs or wears two
eyes before its face, but me:
I could not leave that corpse alone.

I knew it was but tendons,
nerves that twitched beneath the
skin. I knew it could not live
beneath such whacks unless it
be Rasputin or the Lord's own
Foe himself in reptile flesh, I knew,
but still: I'll put it out of its
misery I said. I raised the hoe
and brought it down behind
the head. The snake reared back
and opened wide its toothless mouth.
Down I brought the flat-edged
hoe, and down again.

The flesh bounced back, uncut,
like rubber still, or snails once
in my teeth in Spain. The spit
swelled up inside my mouth.
I raised the hoe. I could not
saw or chop or hack that
bloody corpse in half, but
down I brought the hoe again.

I worked till after dark.

On Sparrowhawk Mountain ~ Don Stinson

Through Oklahoma hills
the river rolls below the rocky point,
cold and green in the thick spring.
Old leaves crackle,
slipping under lovers' feet.

Gouged into stone, names stare:
"J.K. + S.T.,"
"Sigmas #1,"
"Jesus is Love,"
so many words massed here,
simple, senseless joys
falling all over one another,
layers of lust and God
beneath so much sky.

Fish slide through the heavy waters.
Under pale clumps of clouds
a sparrowhawk hovers
against the sun,
feathers of light in its eyes.

Originally appeared in __Flatline Horizon__
Mongrel Empire Press 2018

Because it's Oklahoma ~ Julie Chappell

I

Because it's Oklahoma
and Spring
a warm breeze, lifts the
tenacious, now-dried leaves
of the Blackjack trees with a
gentle lilting breeze, that makes music
with the wind chimes, but soon will become
a raging thunderstorm running rivulets.

Disparate stones of earth eroding.

II

Because it's Oklahoma
and Spring
the scorpions have arisen
from their long winter lethargy
following the delectable spiders
and tender crawling insects
into tiny cracks in the walls and floors.

So far three have died in the attempt.

III

Because it's Oklahoma
and Spring
the rifts in the rocks, fissures in the earth,
ruins of human desire to drain the
red dirt of its oily wealth will bleed
every crawling thing, disturbed, disoriented
fierce with anger at their tormentors.

The aftermath will be terrible.

Potroast and Poetry in Ada ~ Hank Jones

Ken can't join us,
but he says, go to Aldridge's,
get the potroast.
So we do.

Harold, the proprietor, tells us
Ken's a great customer, a fine
poet. Harold has all his books.
Ken's even written
four poems for him.

He brings them out
in a green folder, pulls
a chair up to our table and
reads them to us in a fine,
Oklahoma accent.

One of them is about a
supermoon Harold saw and Ken missed.
Harold told Ken about it.
Ken went home and when he returned
he'd captured the moment for Harold in a poem.

hoping no one sees the tears in my eyes
threatening to run down my cheeks.

The next one Harold reads
Ken wrote after Harold's wife died.
It's a beautiful piece. Harold almost
tears up when he reads it.
I do.
Find myself looking at potroast,
okra, carrots, biscuit,
poking at my plate with my fork,

hoping no one sees the tears in my eyes
threatening to run down my cheeks,

Pony Up - The Last Pit Pony in Oklahoma
~ Markham Johnson

Suzie's lucky, says Grandma, who claimed her cheap
at the Claremore Rodeo, because no fool would bid

on a Shetland with fourteen years of mean staked
to her heart. The last pit pony in Oklahoma, dredged

from the mines, almost blind from years dragging
   wagon-loads
of zinc and lead through the dark. Grandma
   understood—

when you're raised up hard and half wild, kindness
has to force a channel under the skin. Trailered

to Spunky Creek Farm, Dad pulls the pins, drops
the gate, to loose Suzie in the pasture where she'll grow
   tough

and fat on acorns and hay. We're thirteen that summer,
slugging dirt clods and racing chickens around

the barn, when we catch her napping and cull Suzie
from big thoroughbred studs. Cousin Chris climbs

on, legs stuck straight out, kicking his Keds in the air,
  because
he can't reach her ribs, then falls hard. Suzie knows all

the low-branched oak and sycamores she can just
  squeeze
under and the blackberry patch, thick and full

of thorns. This pony, that never loved me, watches
as I slide one leg over her back. Knees hugged to
  heaving sides,

I tuck my head tight to her neck, cool and moist
as a grave, try to be brave, and know I will fail.

But at thirteen you jump aboard, get scraped off
in an Oklahoma summer's red dust, and rise again.

To Myself at 21   ~   Misty Allsup

Saw a picture of [you] today,
>   that faded five-dollar Yankee cap
> that you stapled together
>   because you couldn't bear to throw it away,
> those soft doeskin boots you loved,
>   scuffed and raw-looking,
not an inch of you to spare,
> lines cut deep through your forearms.

[I know: because you work, right?]
> You could never be a board barn princess.
>   *easier than others*

>   Such a bright smile on so sad a face...

I know you better than anyone,
> but I wish I could have seen you
as others saw you –

comfort is depicted, natural
>   throwing a long leg over a colt,
settling into a deep seat like you were melting into those
grooved, leather crevices,
> seen your face tighten as Oklahoma explode
beneath you.

You and you bucking horses
> I wish I could have seen that.
>   *didn't appreciate it*

And, I wish I could have seen you playing the
executive's girl,
> your hair all done up,
>   the result of an insufferable hour at a salon,
in your favorite heels, climbing out of your big truck,
> laughing with the guys at the bar,
>   watching your boyfriend look at spreadsheets,
sipping on a Margarita that lasted all night.

38

Wish I could have seen you
     during all of those days you spent alone
working on the problems no one else wanted to solve,
wearing yourself out,
doing work that made you strong.
Or
driving through the night,
     never stopping for very long,
trying to make that 22 hour drive in 20.

Yeah, I know you better than anyone,
but I still wish I could have seen you then.

Originally published in Green Eggs and Hamlet
Southeastern Oklahoma State University Literary Journal 2017

Strangers on the Prairie ~ Carl Sennhenn

   Distances are diminished
Our universe is smaller than
we knew so now seagulls
whose familiar cries I heard
as a boy in Annapolis roaming
the shores of Chesapeake
Bay and the Atlantic have
followed me to Oklahoma
   Never in early years here
did I listen for any but native
birds whose names I had not learned
Intervening decades have witnessed
changes of all kinds not the least
of which is a landscape altered
by the appearance of lakes
man-made and miles of shoreline
that did not exist when first I came
to a state famous in popular song
for plains swept by dust and wind
and prairies over which hawks fly
but now share airspace with seagulls
These days a generous land of friendly folk
continues to welcome exiles like a sickly
asthmatic brought here to escape the damp
air of coastal climes and as if following
him seagulls far from original
nests find a home they surely
like me gladly claim their own

City of a Survivor Tree ~ Abigail Keegan

Through the window of my earlier life I see the ceiling plaster fall
I hear it hit the floor, the sirens shrill through the city. At times,
the Oklahoma wind sings an aria of memory, it is then,
when alone, with friends, or others, the Gates of Time
force contemplation of the traitors who terrorized everything
a city knew about a life secure in the heart of the heart
of the country. As I age, I look more carefully
on the American Elm that is our city. Random lives
caught in the branches of some greater purpose came together:
citizens rushed to rescue, clearing ash and asphalt, stone
and powdered bone; they pruned broken limbs and branches
repaired and restored life salvaged from a bomb's destruction.
People of Oklahoma City dug deep to open the wounds of roots,
roots that for 100 years had held the tree's life tight against
 ice storms and fierce tornadoes until the assault
of human callousness. The roots drank deeply of the care
needed to revive a battered life, all around the broken city.
we accepted what was needed to patch our houses and our fears.

We made and laid new bricks, churned our cement mixers
while below ground, worms turned and turned the soil
giving us a renewed earth. From skyscrapers to pavement,
together we tended the life of the city, and we nested in its center,
a place for chairs of light above the leaves of grass, beneath
the branches of the survivor Elm, allowing us to believe it could
be possible to go on living for someone else. All around the dead,
like the holy rescue workers, collections of lungs and leaf stomata
banded and breathed together, chlorophyl and hemoglobin
cleaned and gave courage to all the life they could
reviving an exploded city to the strength and stature
of the Survivor Tree. We stand many branches together,
between the Gates of Time, we stand looking back
to our pain, looking forward to thriving as wounded survivors
taking up the Eternal task of raising life above death, even
as the dead sit watching. Winds and hands and doves have dropped
seeds of the Elm at dwellings across the city. From here, seeds
of the surviving Elm have been planted across the Nation. From
here,
we hope you tend them with good hearts, tend them
as if life depends upon their Eternal going on.

Driving Dad to Quadruple Bypass
~ Nathan Gunter

The Ouachita Mountains, where you've come
to live out the end of your life—

    an end
    you've been whittling at for twenty years—

in pre-dawn light are imposing,
tree-lined backs of serpents,
of monsters long spoken of
in hushed whispers
that earn derisive laughs
at church picnics.

These beasts hold back the dawn.
On the prairies where you raised me,
the sun explodes up, the light fills my eyes,
the morning forty weeks pregnant with promise,
great with threat.

Among these beasts, we ride
Arkansas State Highway 8.

Along the road, farm ponds,
the Caddo River, DeGray Lake, and all their arterial
farm creeks
lay, unwaking,
under blankets of fog.

You are quiet in the passenger seat—
in a few hours, they will open
your seventy-nine-year-old chest
and try to give us all more time.

You make a little small talk,
but you're stuttering, using the wrong words,
then falling silent again.

The sun is winning over the Ouachitas.

The fog on the ponds
starts to glow in the light,
starts to rise—

up, up, up,
and then gone.

First Loss ~ Terri Lynn Cummings

I ride my bike as far from home
as I dare. There is no China
with a red lacquer palace
only an invisible border
I do not want to cross

A field of switchgrass holds its breath
at my intrusion. Within the prick of
sandburs and goat heads, tears tell
me to go no further. Here her shadow
slants like a broken promise

Everywhere, scattered examples
of endings—broom weeds
flattened by the soul of music
scrub oaks twisted by fingertips
of dreams

She would have turned seven
played tether ball on baked
clay school yard, chased
ice cream truck at five on Fridays
attended Sunday school with me

All the other lives she should have lived
stolen by cancer hidden in a cloak
of blood and bone. Even if enlightenment
were granted, it would make no difference
A dragon burned my friend to ash

Saliva the Knot ~ Lynn Doiron

I thread my needle. Mama's steel thimbles don't fit
and I suck my own blood from a thumb pricked.

I wore pinafores hand-stitched from flour sacks
with petit flowers, dainty stems, ruffles dusting my
knees.

When the wind blows, faded roses of plastic tangle, roll
to rest on brass markers like weary, antler-locked stags.

The women of my family abide in graves beside their
men,
ceaselessly chatter yea's and nay's through my brain.

Hung from six-count thread ligaments, a swan's
knotted eye
dangles blind. Embroidery gets tee'jus, don't it?

I take back every wrong-headed notion or pricked bleed
ever bled your way, saliva the knot. Anchoring.

Originally published in <u>hand wording</u>
TJMF Publishing 2006

Mt. Scott All-Stars Vs the Milky Way Nine: a Baseball Fantasy   - after BZ (aka, BD)   ~ Todd Fuller

God said
I'm tired of all this
So organized
A ballgame
OKLA vs The Universe
Whoever wins
Gets to live
Otherwise it's dust
To dust since
You're all stardust
Anyway
It's that way for
God once every
5 thousand years
Got to clean
House
The most sacred
Air in OKLA
Is picked to host
At the largest
Corner
Of the Wichita
Mountains
Where it's 1000
Feet down
The lines and
Mt Scott serving as
The pitcher's
Mound & all the
Players stretching
On the field
God decrees

We'll be using
The InterGalactic
League (IGL) rules
Which means 4 not 3
Is the perfect #
Which means 4 outs per
Inning in a 16
Inning game
The managers meet
At home where
They're greeted by
The archangels who'll
Call the game
~~(Smells of)~~ popcorn
& roasted peanuts
Hover 10 feet
Above the crowd
Tensions are high
Astral & terrestrial
Cosmological intentions
Collide & managers
Exchange line up cards
Beneath constellations
Strong Pawnee &
Osage & Kiowa
Aromas drift thru
Concourses
When the Okies take
The field it's a Hall
Of Fame lineup w/
The wily Warren
Spahn on the mtn &

When the interstellar
Leadoff hitter steps
To the plate
It's not the 1st time
An alien touched
Earth yet
The humans all
ooooo and *ahhh* as if
A new word
Has been invented
For death
Or God who
It turns out
Watches from
The Highest
Skybox & after
9 pitches ol' Hooks*
Throws the 1st
Immaculate inning*
Of his career
And every extra-
Terrestrial in
The place oozes
Snot-like crude
Which is the
Customary
Gesture of (alien)
Displeasure & then
The Commerce
Comet* steps
In the box
Only to defy
Gravity for one
Blink of an eye
When he rockets
A ball just shy

Of Meissa* aka
The Shining One
And over the next
6 stanzas the 2
Teams trade
Scoreless frames
Behind Spahn
And Reynolds
In the middle of the 7th
Paid attendance
Is announced
At 1281898*
Meanwhile
At the border
Between the
Atmosphere &
Space 5M
Asylum seekers
Flood Medicine Park
With outlaw*
Hearts & in the top
Of the 9th an
Alien all-star crushes
One to the North Star
Off the boy
from Big Cabin *
who'd been perfect
up 'til then
Making the score
1 to 1 at which
Point ½M Okies
Begin to chant
Bring in Yellow-
*Horse** who begins
Tossing smoke in
The bullpen

47

He relieves
Meal Ticket*
& When the
Pulverizing
Pawnee steps
On Mt Scott
The aliens are all
Astir to see
Someone with a
Laser arm &
Laser eyes atop
The hill it's like
They've never
Seen indigeneity
At work & 6 innings
Later he's still
Mystifying
The Milky Way
Stars
It's becoming one
Of those scrapbook
YouTube Twitter
Moments
W / 20B hits in a day
Just the same
The Mt Scott men
Suffer under the spell
Of wicked alien
Curves from

Unimaginable astral
Angles but in
The bottom of
The 15th it'll be
Pepper Martin* who
Beats out a nubbber
To short & once
The stardust
Clears the Wild
Hoss of the Osage
Touches home
His cosmic journey
Complete & when
Bullet Joe* records
The final out
The score of 2-1
Is surely no surprise
But out beyond
The layers
Of firmament
Silvery edges of
Light make their
Own weightless
Tears & we
All knew they were
Ghosts anyway
Each a sweet breath
Extinguished in
The slightest air

The Lineup Cards:
Milky Way Nine (a)

The Great Slamboris (of)
Blackhole Leather (ss)
Gloaming Galaxy (of)
Supernova Spikes (3b)
Splendid Constellation (c)
Ever Eclipse, aka EE (1b)
Mount Nebula (2b)
Lefty Light-year (of)
Sonic Boom (sp)
Mighty Meteor (p)
Slicing Solar (p)
Tenacious Light (p)
Uncanny Zenith (p)
Marvelous Moony (p)

Mt Scott All-Stars (h)

Bobby Murcer (ss)
Pepper Martin (3b)
Mickey Mantle (of)
Johnny Bench (c)
Willie Stargell (1b)
Paul Waner (of)
Johnny Callison (of)
Jerry Adair (2b)
Warren Spahn (sp)
Allie Reynolds (p)
Ralph Terry (p)
Carl Hubbbell (p)
Mose YellowHorse (p)
Bullet Joe Rogan (p)

Notes:
* Hooks is one of Warren Spahn's nicknames
* Immaculate inning refers to an inning during which a pitcher throws nine pitches (all strikes) to three consecutive batters and records three outs
* The Commerce Comet is Mickey Mantle's nickname
* Meissa refers to a star in the Orion constellation; as the poem suggests, this star has been called the shining one
* 1281898 is an allusion to Mose YellowHorse's birthday
* Medicine Park, Oklahoma (pop. 382, 2010 census) is a vintage cobblestone resort town with a dynamic & notorious past
*Big Cabin, Oklahoma is the birthplace of Ralph Terry
* Mose YellowHorse (Pawnee) played for the Pittsburgh Pirates from 1921-22
* Meal Ticket is Carl Hubbell's nickname
* Pepper Martin (Osage) played for the St. Louis Cardinals from 1928; 1930-1940; and 1944
* Bullet Joe Rogan played in the Negro Leagues with the KC Monarchs from 1920-1938

This ekphrastic poem was inspired by Jim Curran's dad's photos of the Drumright tornado of 1956, posted April 2, 2019, in Forgotten Oklahoma on facebook.

After That ~ Catherine Katey Johnson

Neighbor lady just stood there in her living room
looking out the window frame
staring at her furniture upside down and sideways
in our back yard
she could see it clearly since our house was gone
scattered up the road a bit
left the swamp cooler torn from my bedroom window
hope it still works
hope Daddy can get it hooked up before June
if the house gets put back, that is.

Sanctuary's just a 'tuary now
with that one wall standing
the three pews that remained are out in the open
like they're waiting for someone to raise a revival tent
around them.

Pews or not, they weren't able to revive those five.
Some said we were lucky we didn't lose more.

If you're looking for your roof
I saw three of them lying in the Hampton's front yard.
The brown one's in pretty good shape, considering
but the red one's in parts
more of a do-it-yourself roof kit.
Still trying to figure out how that '53 Buick got up in
that old elm.

TV's all busted to hell but the picture tube's still there.
Maybe it can be salvaged.

Aunt Dottie's kitchen cabinets are still there
drawers are gone   doors all there
no stove, refrigerator, washer
and nothing, not even one can of Vienna Sausage left in
the cupboard.
Bathtub's full of debris
looks like it went sailing through the air
before it took out that redbud.

I ain't seen a house yet left intact.

But I've seen my neighbors
they came by with a thermos of coffee and some
sandwiches
said they'd be back when the tractor got here
to start pulling this stuff into piles
of what can be reused
and what will have to be hauled off
or used for kindling.

Hard to believe it's been sixty-two years since that
terrible twister hit.
These old photos brought it all back, just like it was
yesterday.
Town came back from it pretty good.
We even got a winery now.

Prairie Lore ~ Anne Semple

Beyond the field across the plains,
When prairie grass is amber tanned,
Then comes the smell of autumn rains.

The bunching quail in orchard lanes
Have caught the scent the grass has fanned
Beyond the field across the plains.

Along with flocks of restless cranes,
Whose anxious wails disturb the land,
There comes the smell of autumn rains.

At dusk the clinging air remains
To form a wispy yellow band
Beyond the field across the plains.

To men who eye the weather vanes
And know to read a shifting hand,
There comes the smell of autumn rains.

The guinea-hen, as daylight wanes,
Protests so all may understand –
Beyond the field across the plains
There comes the smell of autumn rains.

Originally published in Prairie-Born
Kaleidograph Press 1942
Reprinted with permission of Janie Semple Umstead

PAINTING OKLAHOMA ~ Jennifer Kidney

This subtle landscape pleases the painter's eye:
dusty greens, shades of mauve and russet,
gentle hills resembling burial mounds.
These prairies once were Indian hunting grounds.
Now, as summer ends, only the sun singes the grass
yet smoke pervades the air like a ghost.
Natives harvest gold from the red earth
where the painter sees unnatural eruptions
of tiny towns and sprawling farms.
To the east, hues of green increase.
In the west, eroded into mesas and ravines,
the sky blushes and spreads a palette
of flame and ash. The darkening sky explodes
into frozen fireworks overhead
as the painter packs up tubes and brushes
and furls the landscape into darkness.

Originally published in Red Earth Review,
July 2019

Red Earth Redress ~ Cullen Whisenhunt

colors, history

Oklahoma
Okla humma
"Red people"
Rednecks
hillbillies, pig farmers, cattle ranchers,
hay haulers, deer hunters, gun toters
Red-headed, red-handed, red-eyed
dope smokers, crack dealers, and meth cookers
Bad Breakers
Broken promises in the Promised Land
Canaanites proudly wearing the buckle of the Bible Belt
in God's country
FUCK Texas
"Red River rivals"
Crimson and cream smokes burnt orange any day
Boomer Sooner, Boomer Sooner
Boomer Sooner Schooners sailed red dirt oceans
and weighed anchor at boondocks
Where Deliverance descendants set up shop with banjos
and shotgun weddings and Confederate flags
and dead Indians and capitalist blood money
and became religiously racist, radical, right-wing,
Republicans
I mean, red state, right?

Wrong
…ish

Sure, Tulsa's arts district has tried to whitewash
over the good ole days when oil barons,
barrel racing, and race riots were all the rage,
When brown faces turned black and blue and the violet
night sky was splashed red orange by burning black
gold.

can't do things on Sundays

And yes, some blue law believers are still fighting
rainbows
and pink triangles while their own hometowns
are so far in the red that no amount of blood money
can keep greengrocers from blacking out windows.
But down on the Red River, dead Indians now paint
with all the colors of the windfall at Windstar and
Choctaw,
Where greens, silvers, and coppers return to them
straight from the pink and purple purses of blue-haired
white ladies.
Up in the city, black jazz and blues roots show that
invisible men
can at least leave musical footprints,
And of course, if you listen closely, these Oklahoma hills
still echo Woody Guthrie lyrics about blue collar
worker's rights
and damn near Red Machine Communism,
In fact, just look skyward, and at the hills and valleys,
at the plains and creeks and soil and bedrock,
And you'll see there's no state bluer, greener, or more
golden,
and all of it growing out of red, white, and black.

*Originally published as "Color Poem" in Red Earth Review, no. 6
(July 2018)*

Mountain Kings ~ Leah Chaffins

My father cast his line again on the opposite shore.
His inner tube floated in the dark shadows
Where catfish crawled the murk under the loom
Of Mt. Sheridan. Warm green water waked 'round
My face. Medicine Creek kissed cool sun-red
Cheeks that seemed to crackle with each smile.
My three year old legs kicked against weighted
Nothingness, dipping into cooler currents.
Here was only solitude,
A father, and his child, a place
Where heroes were made, and fears disappeared
In the iridescence of a dragon fly's wings.

This was not the Medicine Creek of the tourists, but
further
North, before the waters snaked Saddle Mountain's
Bed, miles from where sightseers walked cobblestone
Paths, stealing rocks as souvenirs to be laid in urban
Flowerbeds as if cast down by the gods to rest
Ornately beneath the bobbing heads of zinnias and day
lilies.

But back there, that didn't matter. All the mattered
Was the sun's journey across the sky until it slowly
Crowned the mountain in gold. Pink
Skies faded to purple as father hunched
On the shore throwing fish heads into the water,
A cigarette gripped between his teeth.

I sat in the sand, a can of Coke-a-cola between
My legs as fireflies became fairies, and the moon's
Reflection proved the now clear black water
Held magic. A small fire cackled embers
Shot to the heavens before disappearing
In a bed of stars. The night's diamonds twinkled as
Frogs and cicadas hummed enchantments
To heavy-hooded eyes that blinked back sleep,
A fruitless battle to make the moment into
Forever. On Medicine Creek, treading water is
Seeking magic beneath the cloak of the mundane,
God wears a father's face, and shadows are
The work of Mountain Kings.

Homesteading ~ Randy Prus

I came to love,
the redbud, late March,
still asked after twenty years,
"so you ain't from around here?"

I was fixin' to tell 'im I'd absorbed
the idioms and rhythms,
the sound of the single finger wave,
& the call to Jesus meeting,
the smell of bar-b-que, catfish
frying, the bawls of young cows,
frog legs, a kind of football,
snow, new, rain rare....
...but then I remembered ants,
spider bites, hail and fire, a boy
murdered by a someone,
standing his ground, how
quickly place dissolves to memory...

I decided it best to be here,
but not from here...I talk funny,
but listen just the same.

No Reservations ~ Jill Hawkins

when you're born
in Oklahoma and you're not
an Indian, you only belong
to your parents

the wheat only waves
its feathery tips to the sky
and rose rocks form like pecans
under your neighbor's tree

and daddy's side never really left
the leaning house at Center Point
where postcards pinned to curtains
meant someone got beyond the creek line

staying didn't make them Native
with cheekbones close to the eye
just Okies, belly crawling
in crop fields, biting turnips sometimes
as they'd rise

Originally published in Southwestern American Literature
(Fall, 2015).

How Much of Heaven ~ John Morris

The way the cold decants the air
into a truer blue under January sun,
wrings the atmospheric haze
dry, crisps oxygen, and mounts
whip-like tree limbs into
a mid-winter frame lit by
a dazzle of light after your waste
of too many good minutes--
should not all of creation look like this?

Don't you stand taller, more
erect than usual, as if in some
boot camp, eyes fixed,
straining to hear instructions
that are certain to follow
the raucous jabber of starlings?
Shouldn't you snap your right arm
into a salute as spectral glare
rushes your mind in a honeyed flood?
How much gospel can you
be prepared to offer up while
there is still time to sing?

And a steady pavane of moments
has paraded unnoticed past your eyes
since you sat in the front seat
while your irritable father stewed
about taking you on his drive out
to cuss with his military cronies
and, supposedly, fly radio-controlled
model airplanes. You recall only
the ride, squirming in the seat,
quietly, when your father punched

on the radio. Knowing any
noise would result in furious rant,
you focused your soul into three notes
that began that network news broadcast.
Whatever happened to those tones
and the news that gray afternoon?
And the empty lot that has since
sprouted beige rows of apartments
in a leukemia of construction business?
Into what far field have the planes
flown with your father, now smaller
(continued with no break)

than life and his outsized voice
squeezed out by eternity?

And whatever are you to make
of your wife's shallow breathing
and her open mouth as she curls
within a snug anaesthetic blanket
following a routine procedure
and resists your attempts
to rouse her until the nurse
adds liquid to her drip
and roughly shakes her awake?
What wonders was she ripped away
from and is there any light left
here as she blinks and readjusts
to the usual piths and wisps?
How much of heaven can any of us
afford listlessly to ignore?

Oklahoma, Considered ~ Paul Juhasz

David Foster Wallace tells us to consider the lobster.
And we should. But not for the reasons he says. Instead,
we should marvel that this creature, this armored,
weaponed monster from the deep is something we eat.
How in the actual hell did that happen? How
unaccountable that someone in the long-ago saw a
lobster, hideous, bottom-feeding fiend, and said "I'm
going to draw some butter and eat that motherfucker,"
rather than worrying about the safety of his children, of
his friends and family, of his very soul.

And while we're on the subject, consider bleu cheese?
How did that happen? At least the lobster is an
animated, living thing. But bleu cheese? A disk of
piebald rot. Who the hell first thought, "I wonder if that
festering circle of decay is tasty?" It must have been a
bet; a "hold my beer and watch this" moment.

Or consider the coconut. Such a perfect food, really.
The antioxidant-rich water inside is perfect for re-
hydration, the milk silky and rich. If you chip off a
piece of its wooly shell, you can use that as a utensil to
scrape out the coconut's luscious meat. The coconut,
when you consider it, is a self-contained place setting. A
perfect nugget the world has created to feed us. And
then placed in a tree 70 feet tall. With no branches.

There is instruction in such things: The world will nourish in unanticipated forms, in unpredictable ways, at unexpected times. This lesson strikes me as I stand beneath an endless sky and consider Oklahoma. After a twenty-two-year marriage has been drained of all love, as I stand exiled from an old garden in search of a new, I do not marvel that it is this land I'm drawn to. Not New Haven, where I was born and raised; not Texas, where I lived for fifteen years, not Pennsylvania, the false Eden from which I'm banished, but Oklahoma, a land I've visited maybe a dozen times at most.

Here, the wind acknowledges suffering, whispers healing and defiance. I will fill my lungs with it. Here, the warmth enfolds, embraces, rejuvenates. I shall let it burn my skin. Here, the red earth absorbs pain like a sponge. I shall offer it my sweat, take it beneath my fingernails. Here, I sense a spirit. I nod to It, and It nods to me. "Be at peace," It tells me, and I let that peace flow through me, filling me with hope, erasing doubt until the only question left to consider is:

Where in Oklahoma can I get a good lobster? Preferably in a coconut-cream sauce. The dressing I'd like on my salad should be obvious.

Before Market ~ Cathy Miller

like dawn wraiths they gather in early cool
to pick the peas the beans fresh corn
a baby still asleep on the truck seat
they walk the rows filling their sacks and boxes
the black dirt silky velvet on their feet
a robin pulls a worm   dew damp on the leaves
in the field across the way a rooster calls

Oklahoma Seasons ~ Bill Boudreau

Spring:
Melted snow on somber soil,
As if in communion,
Purifies the land,
Dew rinses winter dust,
Tempests on the horizon,
Southwest, thunder rolls,
Wind sweeps rolling hills,
Harsh funnels stir all at rest,
Storm passes, broken sky,
Sun beams a new dawn,
Amid calm, stems bud,
Creation's rainbows rise,
Conceptions in red earth,
Floras in labor, give birth,
Passion excites pairs in union,
Resurrection on the terrain,
Shoots emit scented flowers,
Life pervades the Plains,
Bloom rise in majestic colors,
Advent of Oklahoma Spring.

Summer:
Immaculate sky canopies Prairies,
Above, the lazy sun arcs the day,
And radiates intense heat on Plains,
Sunset aflame, blazes last glimmer,
Points of light sprinkle firmament,
Coyotes howls chill the night,
Tumbleweeds roll at will,
In twilight's stillness we hear,
Echoes of the past over swelling hills,
Tribes' rain dance, far and near,
On distant range, cowboys yodel,

Herding cattle to greener pastures,
Coiled rattlers sunbathe on rocks,
Cicadas break silent stillness,
Dry grass, trees camouflage nature,
Heat of summer, landscape in frenzy,
Nature reaches maturity,
Growing energy, begins to fade,
Facing burn-out, meets amber of Fall.

Fall:
Faded colors carpet red earth,
Wind sweeps dust off grasslands,
Skeletal limbs releasing leaves,
Naked trees, mark of scarcity
In silent grace, monarchs glide,
Flowers devoid of nectar,
Cicadas echo in arid days,
Birds flock for long journeys,
Plains mourn loss of life,
Fields expose callus wounds,
Lakes' vapor rises to clouds,
Pairs go separate ways,
Offspring on first journey,
Life prepares hibernation,
Evidence of white famine,
Early sunsets, nature's notice,
A cold stillness to descend.

Winter:
Late sunrise, early sunset,
Northwest wind gusts,
Drizzle carpets the grass,
Trees, fields entombed in glass,
Sun deflects prismatic colors,
Slow rhythmic drips,
Shift of wind from the South,
A false Spring air,
Red earth in cotton drifts,
Melt away as sun passes,
North front blows,
Nature in indecision,
Warm mild days, a paradox,
Sun and snow in contention,
Buddings eager to sprout,
Freeze descends on pastures,
Tells it's not time to come out,
Stillness on fading colors,
Life's energy in submission,
Some forever, others in hibernation,
Awaiting reincarnation.

Indian Paintbrushes ~ Ron Wallace

Flowers grow
>	flickers of orange fire
dancing on green fields under Oklahoma skies.
Like weeds
>	they hold to the worst terrain
and spread everywhere.

They beautify discarded Coors cans
and swarm beneath barbed wire
>	filling empty cattle pastures,
piercing coyote bones
taken by the grass
on land where, long ago,
Choctaw and Chickasaw hunted.

Once,
as a boy,
I worked the roots of a handful loose
>	from the rocky soil
across the gravel road,
running in front of my house
and brought them to my mother's flower beds.

With all the care a ten year old could muster,
I replanted the fire
between the petunias and the four o'clocks.
But there
>	among the tame flowers
>		soon
>			they perished.

"They grow wild;
that's just how some things are meant to be,"
Momma said
as she watered her carefully tended garden
in the summer heat of Oklahoma.

But always
    without fail,
before she'd go back inside,
she would walk over to the edge of our yard
and look across the dusty road
    at the fiery red-orange blanket,
        burning in the last light of day.

Originally published in <u>Native Son</u>
TJMF Publishing 2006

August: Osage County ~ Howard Starks

Dust hangs heavy on the dull catalpas;
the cicadas are scraping interminably
       at the heat-thickened air –
   no rain in three weeks, no real breeze all day.
In the dim room,
   the blinds grimly endure the deadly light,
      protecting the machined air,
as the watchers watch the old lady die.

"I'm eighty-six," she said; "it's high time –
      now John's gone."
     And to the town's new doctor,
"You're a good boy" (she had a great-grandson
   who was older), "so don't fiddle around.
  When fighting was needed, I fought –
      but I'm all fought out."
and later –
"John left when he was due – well – I'm due now."
     "I promise," he whispered;
      "I've learned when right is right."

Now her daughters sit – and her granddaughters –
   and at night her grandsons –
      and her pampered sons-in-law.
    One of these, not known for eloquence –
or tears – said last week,
      "Ola, chance gave me a mother
  but God gave me two."
      She smiled at that,
   "Yes, I had one boy; God gave me seven more."

She lies under the sheet,
    thin as one of her old kitchen knives,
    honed by years and use to fragile sharpness,
    but too well-tempered to break just yet.

It's two days since she spoke –
                  "Don't cry, Bessie;
          puppies just die, that's all."
            (A girl again
          gentling baby sister.)

          All the watchers can do
    is wipe her dry mouth with gentle wetness.
They watch her old hands and murmur –
         How many biscuits
           and pans of gravy?
         How many babies soothed
           and bee stings daubed with bluing?
         How many lamp wicks trimmed?
         How many berries picked?
                  words circling
as her quiet breath winds down to silence.

No sobs, for she was due, but tears, a few,
       selfish ones,
         before the calls, the "arrangements"
      to put her to bed, beside John
            on the dusty hilltop.
Standing there,
    we look up from the dry clods
    and the durable grey stone,
upwards –
  expectantly –
    westwards –
        where the clouds grow dark.

Contributors

- Dorothy Alexander -- Whose life is stained by the wild plums in the short-grass country of the Cheyenne-Arapaho Nation of western Oklahoma
- Sly Alley – 2016 Oklahoma Book Award for *Strong Medicine*
- Misty Allsup – From the backroads of Bryan County Oklahoma to the mountains of Wyoming
- Rilla Askew – Oklahoma Writer's Hall of Fame, 1998 & 2007 Oklahoma Book Awards, 2001 American Book Award,
- Paul Austin – From the lights of Broadway to the hills of Oklahoma
- Jim Barnes – 2009-2010 Oklahoma Poet Laureate – 1993 Oklahoma Book Award winner
- Bill Boudreau – An Acadian poet living in OKC
- Paul Bowers - Lives and writes in the rural wilds of Major County, Oklahoma.
- Nathan Brown – Oklahoma Poet Laureate 2013-2014 - Oklahoma Book Award 2009
- Leah Chaffins – Cameron University, Lawton, Oklahoma
- Julie Chappell -- Lady of the Lake in Pawnee County, Oklahoma
- Terri Lynn Cummings -- The bard from Tulsa, Stephens, Payne, & Oklahoma Counties
- Richard Dixon – A poetic mind who hangs out in Edmond, Oklahoma playing a little tennis
- Lynn Doiron – Oklahoma expatriate living in Baja, California
- Todd Fuller – Poet, Curator, Western History Collections - University of Oklahoma
- Larry Griffin -- of Flint Creek in Oklahoma, Cherokee Nation, where he watches eagles fish.
- Nathan Gunter – Editor of *Oklahoma Today*, sixth generation Okie

- Ken Hada -- A poet often perched on the back deck in Pottawatomie County
- Carol Hamilton - Poet Laureate of Oklahoma 1995-1997 and Poet Laureate for the 50th anniversary of Midwest City and Tinker AFB.
- Joy Harjo – Poet Laureate of the United States - 1995 and 2003 Oklahoma Book Awards
- Jessica Isaacs -- Director of Seminole State College Howlers & Yawpers Symposium, 2015 Oklahoma Book Award
- Catherine Katey Johnson – Proud Okie from the First Families in the Territory
- Markham Johnson - Somehow the winds swept me back to Tulsa
- Hank Jones -- Newly transplanted, putting Down roots on the shore of Lake Keystone
- Paul Juhasz – The prose poet of Mesta Park
- Abigail Keegan – Oklahoma City, Oklahoma - Professor Emerita at Oklahoma City University.
- Jennifer Kidney – Poet - The University of Oklahoma in Norman, Oklahoma
- Chuck Ladd – From the Shadow of Sugarloaf Mountain in Bryan County
- Louis L'Amour – The king of the American Western ~ 1984 Presidential Medal of Freedom
- Sharon Edge Martin – A freshwater fish in the salty waters of Creek County
- Bill McCloud – Ponca City poet and the Wild Horse of the Osage
- Wilma Elizabeth McDaniel – An Oklahoma expatriate in California from Stroud, Oklahoma
- Cathy Miller – OKC poet from The University of Central Oklahoma

- Jeanetta Calhoun Mish – Oklahoma Book Award ~ 2010, Poet Laureate of Oklahoma 2017-2019
- N. Scott Momaday – Kiowa Pulitzer Prize winner, Poet Laureate of Oklahoma 2007-2008
- John Moreland – Tulsa singer/songwriter, a poet of lyrics
- John Morris – Poet and professor at Cameron University in Lawton, Oklahoma
- Benjamin Myers – Oklahoma's Poet Laureate 2016-2017 - Oklahoma Book Award ~ 2011
- Randy Prus – Southeastern Oklahoma State U.
- Ann Semple – Of the Choctaw Nation - Poet Laureate of Oklahoma 1944-1945
- Carl Sennhenn – Oklahoma Poet Laureate 2001-2002, Oklahoma Book Awards 2007 and 2011
- Sandra Soli -- Once a traveling teaching artist and editor, now a poet living in Edmond, Ok.
- Jim Spurr – The Poet Laureate of Shawnee, Oklahoma; he lived out loud.
- Howard Starks – The sage of Southeastern Oklahoma State University
- Don Stinson – Northeastern Oklahoma University professor and poet
- Ron Wallace – From the Eastside of Durant, Oklahoma to Morrison Hall at Southeastern
- Cullen Whisenhunt – Born, raised, and supposedly educated in Bryan County.
- John Yozzo – First generation Okie from Ponca City, Oklahoma